FIGHTING VEHICLES OF THE RED ARMY

B. PERRETT

FIGHTING VEHICLES OF THE RED ARMY

ARCO PUBLISHING COMPANY INC.
New York, New York

Published by ARCO PUBLISHING COMPANY, Inc.
219 Park Avenue South, New York, N.Y. 10003

Library of Congress Catalog Card Number 70–118998
ISBN 0–668–02340–6

*Printed in Great Britain
by A. Wheaton & Co., Exeter*

Contents

Abbreviations

AFV	Armoured Fighting Vehicle
AP	Armour Piercing
APBC	Armour Piercing Ballistic Capped
APC	Armoured Personnel Carrier
APDS	Armour Piercing Discarding Sabot
APHE	Armour Piercing High Explosive
HE	High Explosive
HVAP	Hyper Velocity Armour Piercing
ICBM	Inter-Continental Ballistic Missile
NATO	North Atlantic Treaty Organization
UAR	United Arab Republic

Acknowledgements

I SHOULD like to acknowledge most gratefully the assistance I have received from Mr Gerard Dooley, with particular reference to the research he has carried out on T100. I should also like to thank the Curator, RAC Tank Museum; the Photographic Librarian, Imperial War Museum; the Military Attache's office, Embassy of Israel, and the staffs of AP, UPI and the Radio Times Hulton Picture Library for their help in supplying the illustrations contained in this book. My greatest debts, however, have been incurred when the work has bogged down in most difficult going, only to be recovered by the unfailing encouragement provided by my wife.

Preface

MY INTENTIONS in writing this book have been twofold. Firstly, to provide a guide to the development of the Red Army's fighting vehicles in one cover, and in so doing fill a gap for serious students of the subject, who, unless they are prepared to delve very deeply, must resort to a few publications in German and Russian. Secondly, to demonstrate that whilst the Red Army may well be the Bogyman of the Free World, any Bogyman loses a lot of his terror if it is known that he suffers from, shall we say, arthritis, however big his stick.

I do not pretend that this survey represents a complete history of the development of Russian Armour. A few vehicles, such as T46 and the BA series of armoured cars, have been omitted, simply because their development either has no bearing on the main theme, or because they contributed nothing worthwhile to the technology of their time.

My analysis of the vehicles used in the various branches of the Soviet Armoured Corps has been compiled with a view to demonstrating the development of the strengths and weaknesses of Russian design and practice, rather than the amassment of a vast number of statistics, although of course figures have been included where they are relevant.

B. PERRETT

August, 1969

CHAPTER I

Early Days

THE CONDITIONS facing the Russian Imperial Army on the Eastern Front 1914–1917 were very different from those prevailing on the Western Front. In the East, advances were measured in hundreds of miles, rather than thousands of yards. The Brusilov Offensive proved that, properly supported, a breakthrough was possible. There was still a limited role for cavalry.

There was, therefore, less urgency in the East for the solving of the machine gun and barbed wire problem which was causing deadlock in the West. Indeed, the British solution, the tank, could not have been within the productive capacity of the creaking Russian industry, even if the problem had been urgent.

Not that armour was entirely unknown in the Czar's Armies. Shortly before the outbreak of war, a number of armoured cars had been ordered from France, and during the war, Great Britain supplied armoured cars including Austin and Peerless models. Naturally, these machines were only capable of undertaking local operations, and their effect on the overall position was negligible, although their individual performances were impressive.

After the Revolution, the Western Allies ceased their aid to the Russian Government, and when the Civil War broke out, supplied the Whites with British Mark Vs and Whippets, and French Renault FTs and St Chamonds. These naturally fell into the hands of the Reds and formed the first armoured units of the Red Army.

It was in 1919 that the Red Army produced its first tank, based upon and closely resembling the Renault FT. This was known as the M17, and given the courtesy title of "Freedom Fighter Comrade Lenin".

The Reds of course had little idea of the tactical and strategic usages of armour, and their technology was limited. In addition, spares for the captured British and French vehicles must have been in critically short supply, but somehow these were kept running for some time after the end of the Civil War.

However, the Russians were very willing to learn, and began to look abroad for their ideas. The prestige of the French Army at the time was unjustifiably enormous and as the French had finished the Great War with a vast stock of tanks, mostly the small Renault FTs, they were considered to be the experts on armour. The French theory that tanks should be subordinate to the Infantry was almost universally accepted and, lacking in

[Radio Times Hulton Picture Lib

Peerless Armoured Car, with group of revolutionaries: Moscow, October 1917

[Radio Times Hulton Picture Library

M17: the first Russian tank, 1919

experience as they were, the Russians followed the French lead.

The Civil War had left the country bankrupt and industrially exhausted, and it was not until after 1925 that a fresh design left the drawing board and went into production.

This was the T18, also known as MS1, and was a much improved version of the M17. The vehicle, like the M17, was armed with a short 37mm gun and a co-axially mounted mg, and carried a crew of two. At 10½mph it was twice as fast as M17. The vehicle retained the "tail" feature attached to its rear which had been fitted to the FT design to improve its obstacle crossing capacity. The weight of the vehicle was 5½ tons, rather less than M17.

In 1929 T18 saw service during the East China Railway incident, but was phased out of service shortly afterwards.

Although improved versions known as MSII and MSIII were produced, the vehicle was hopelessly out of date by Western standards and offered very little more than its World War I parent.

In 1927 the Soviet Union produced the T23 tankette, weighing only 4 tons and carrying one mg. This resembled a small armoured box on a tracked chassis, and was not a success.

In 1930 the Russians' first attempt to build a medium tank was also a failure. This was the T14, the general design of which was similar to contemporary Western tanks. The vehicle was ambitiously armed, having a 76mm gun, and is the first indication of the Russians' great interest in gun power. The suspension was far from satisfactory and doubtless automotive problems were experienced. In view of its 19-ton weight, relatively large size and general appearance, armoured protection appears to have been inadequate.

[Radio Times Hulton Picture Library

Austin-Putilov armoured half-track in May Day Parade, 1922

[RAC Tank Museum

T27: Russian tankette based on Carden-Lloyd Mk VI

A year later another tankette appeared under the title of T27. This was a direct copy of the British Carden-Lloyd MkVI tankette. The vehicle weighed 3 tons and was powered by a 4 cylinder engine which was capable of driving it at 26mph. It carried a two-man crew, each of whom was provided with individual head covers in the form of truncated armour pyramids. Armour thickness was 7mm and one machine gun was carried.

The trouble with tankettes, of course, was that whilst they might be very useful against troops in the open, as far as the armoured battle was concerned, they could not even knock each other out, whilst they were at the mercy of any other AFV on the battlefield, provided it mounted something heavier than a machine gun, and they soon ceased to be fashionable in serious armies.

Up to this time, total Russian tank production was numbered in hundreds, but 1929 saw a turning point in the Soviet attitude to armour and from then on design, development and manufacture of AFVs gathered momentum. At one stage the Russians even permitted the Germans to establish a secret experimental station in Russia as Germany was not allowed tanks under the terms of the Versailles Treaty, and hoped to profit in experience thereby, but the Germans provided little or no practical help.

Russian designers had, perforce, to rely upon designs from Britain and the United States for their ideas and translated these successfully into a formidable series of fighting vehicles, incorporating many of their own concepts.

At first the way was difficult and many mistakes were made, but the foundation of many Soviet designs for the 1940s and 1950s was laid in this period.

[Imperial War Museum

T27 in course of construction

CHAPTER 2

Light Tanks

T26

MARK A	CREW:	Commander/Gunner, Gunner, Driver
	WEIGHT:	8.5 tons
	SPEED:	18.7mph
	ARMOUR:	15mm
MARK B	CREW:	Commander, Gunner, Driver
	WEIGHT:	9.4 tons
	SPEED:	17.5mph
	ARMOUR:	15mm
MARK C	CREW:	Commander, Gunner, Driver
	WEIGHT:	10.3 tons
	SPEED:	17mph
	ARMOUR:	25mm max

THE BRITISH FIRM of Vickers has always pursued, even up to the present day, an independent line of thought on the question of fighting vehicle development, despite the discouragement of those in power. Their development of the Six Ton light tank in the closing years of the 'twenties was received by the War Office coldly, although the vehicle was a better proposition than the Carden-Lloyd light tanks of the day.

Other countries, however, could not afford the luxury of scepticism, and the vehicle was purchased by the Russians, amongst others, in 1931. The Russians found that it satisfied their requirements to such an extent that they immediately put it into mass production, under the title of T26.

The first production model, known as T26A, followed the early British models in having two small machine gun turrets, but as this type of armament made the vehicle no more useful than a large tankette, a single turret version mounting a high velocity 45mm gun, was produced, with a co-axially mounted mg. This version was known as T26B and fought on the Communist side during the Spanish Civil War. A later version, T26C, was produced to offset the defects found inherent in the earlier mark on active service. In the main, these improvements brought about a better distribution of armour, and better visual equipment.

The T26 series was driven by a petrol engine capable of producing the speeds required for reconnaissance and flank protection. The drive sprocket was at the front, and the suspension consisted of two four-wheel bogies each side, mounted on pivoting arms, being reinforced by a pair of heavy leaf springs on each bogie. Four top rollers returned the track to the rear idler.

T26 also saw service in Manchuria and Finland and was still active as late as 1942.

[RAC Tank Museum

T26A and T26B

[Imperial War Museum

T26C: an unusual shot of British and Russian troops operating together; Persia, 1941

THE EARLY AMPHIBIANS
T37 – T38 – T40

The development of these interesting little vehicles was based upon the British Carden-Lloyd A4 E11. Their role was that of reconaissance, and for their time they represented a very advanced appreciation of the capability of armour.

T37 appeared in 1933, T38 in 1936 and T40 in 1940. They weighed respectively 3 tons, 4 tons and 6 tons. Armament was sacrificed for the benefit of mobility, and in each case consisted of a single machine gun. Armour was sufficient only to keep out small arms fire. The vehicles carried a crew of two, the commander in a tiny turret on the right, the driver immediately to his left. The engine compartment was at the rear, although the drive sprocket was mounted forward. Suspension was of the Carden-Lloyd type, consisting of a pair of two wheel bogies per side, except for T40 which had a torsion bar suspension mounting four road wheels per side. All vehicles had a rear idler, and top rollers, two in the case of T37 and T38, and three for T40. Buoyancy tanks were built in and as no further proofing was required, the vehicles could take to the water at will. When immersed, propulsion was by means of a screw which could

[Imperial War Museum

T40

[Imperial War Museum

T37 Driver under instruction—note rescue boat!

produce a speed of 4 knots in calm water, although the low freeboard must have caused concern even in choppy water.

Apart from the adoption of torsion bar suspension in T40, external differences between the vehicles consisted largely of rearrangement of the flotation tanks to counteract improvements

[Imperial War Museum

T38

[Imperial War Museum

T38's rudder and propeller

in armoured protection, and the resultant increase in weight as the original T37 design was developed.

T38 became the first air-portable AFV when it was experimentally lashed below the belly of a four-engined bomber.

T60 – T70 – T80

T60 made its appearance in 1940 as the light tank of the Red Army's modernisation plan. The chassis consisted of four single road wheels per side mounted on torsion bars, with a rear idler and three top return rollers. The drive sprocket was at the front. The vehicle was driven by a 6-cylinder petrol engine of 85hp, which could move its 8½-ton weight at 28mph.

Armoured protection was limited to 15mm maximum, and the armament consisted of a 20mm cannon. The crew consisted of a driver and a commander/gunner.

In action the vehicle was found to be ineffective, and was redesigned rapidly to carry a 45mm gun on a strengthened chassis, the latter having the addition of another pair of road wheels. In this form it was designated T70. The crew was still

[Imperial War Museum

T60

[RAC Tank Museum

T70

limited to two, inhibiting the vehicle's performance either in a fighting or a reconnaissance role. The gun, although an improvement, left a great deal to be desired, and a further modification was obviously necessary if the reconnaissance troops were not to become seriously demoralised.

This took the form of the provision of an improved two-man turret mounting a 76.2mm gun, but T80, as the vehicle was designated, was almost stillborn, as by the time of its production reconnaissance was becoming the responsibility of the more formidable and better-protected T34/76.

The failure of this generation of light tanks severely shook the Red Army's confidence in this type of vehicle, and it was not until 1955, twelve years later, that the next light tank was introduced.

PT76

CREW:	Commander/Gunner, Loader, Driver
ARMAMENT:	1 × 76.2mm or 1 × 85mm gun, 1 × 7.62mm co-axial mg
WEIGHT:	16 tons
LENGTH:	22ft 0in
WIDTH:	10ft 3in
HEIGHT:	7ft 4in
SPEED:	31mph – 6 knots
ARMOUR:	40mm maximum

The realisation in the early 1950s that reconnaissance is best performed by vehicles designed primarily for this role turned the attention of Russian designers once again to the light tank.

The Red Army had indicated a requirement for a vehicle which possessed a high degree of mobility, including an amphibious capacity, a reasonable degree of protection, and a sufficiently powerful weapon to get it out of trouble if the need arose. It is interesting to note that at this particular juncture, NATO's plans for the defence of Western Europe were based upon the defence of a series of river lines, and such a design cannot have been called for purely as a matter of coincidence.

The PT76 first took its place in the Reconnaissance Units in 1955. It is a first class vehicle for its intended role, and has no counterpart in Western armies. Its boat-shaped hull is equipped with built-in buoyancy, and has a large ground clearance. The chassis consists of six pairs of wheels moulded with a chrysanthemum pattern, suspended from torsion bars. The drive sprocket is at the rear, and the idler forward. There are no top rollers. The vehicle is driven on land by a 320hp diesel engine with a clutch and brake steering system, and in the water is propelled and steered by two high-powered water jets, situated in the stern. When not in use, these jets are closed by pivoting flaps. The intakes for the water propulsion unit are situated in the hull sides, above the catwalk, level with the rearmost road wheel.

The turret, resembling an upturned soup bowl, has a flat top with a one-piece hatch for the commander and loader, into which recesses for vision blocks have been moulded for the commander. The one-piece hatch cannot be anything but a disadvantage, as it opens forward, thus limiting vision when not closed down. The driver's hatch is situated amidships immediately below the mantlet, the driver being provided with three episcopes for closed running.

The gun is an adaption of the well tried 76.2mm gun with a long muzzle brake, and is 48 calibres long. An experimental version of the vehicle had an 85mm gun with a fume extractor and conventional muzzle brake, being known in this form as PT85.

[RAC Tank Museum

PT76: gun traversed rear

CHAPTER 3

Medium Tanks

including Light Medium BT Series

T28

CREW:	Commander, Gunner, Loader, Driver, 2 Machine Gunners
ARMAMENT:	1 × 76.2mm gun; 3–4 × 7.62mm mg.
WEIGHT:	28 tons
ARMOUR:	36mm maximum
SPEED:	27mph
INTRODUCED:	1935

IN 1932, at the time that the design for this vehicle was conceived, Soviet designers were still examining what the world had to offer and incorporating the best in their own designs. In common with the armies of the West, as distinct from the German Army, the Soviet Army was bedevilled with the Infantry Tank theory as well as the theory of all round action, and although the Russians succumbed less to the first dogma than their British, French and American counterparts, their belief in the second was profound throughout the greater part of the 1930s.

The vehicle which impressed Soviet designers to a great degree was the British A1E1 Independent with its 47mm main armament mounted in the main turret, surrounded by four subsidiary machine gun turrets and whilst Independent was more faithfully copied in T35, T28 shows a distinct family likeness.

The vehicle was carried on the same multiplicity of small road wheels (12 per side) although the number of top return rollers was limited to four. A pair of reserve road wheels was mounted on either side of the engine decks. Large side plates protected the lower hull and suspension.

Power was supplied by a V12 petrol engine of 500hp producing a top speed of 27mph which represented an adequate return on a vehicle weighing 25 tons. Like Independent, the main armament was housed in the major of the turrets. This was a 76.2mm gun only 16.5 calibres long producing a very low muzzle velocity, mounted co-axially with a 7.62mm mg. Later marks were fitted with a gun 26 calibres long, remedying this

[Imperial War Museum

T28

defect to a limited extent. Two further 7.62mm mgs were housed in subsidiary turrets respectively to the right and left and forward of the main turret.

The vehicle remained the standard Russian medium tank until 1941, by which time it was hopelessly outclassed by the German Panzers.

THE BT SERIES

CREW:	Commander, Driver, Gunner
ARMAMENT:	1 × 37mm or 1 × 45mm or 1 × 76.2mm gun
LENGTH:	18ft 0in
WIDTH:	7ft 4in
HEIGHT:	7ft 6in
SPEED:	69mph on wheels, 37mph on tracks
ARMOUR:	15mm

It is not quite true to say that the American Walter Christie was a prophet entirely without honour in his own country, but it is rather bitter reflection that his ideas should have formed the basis of so many successful tank designs for the army of a country opposed to capitalism and free enterprise in any form.

Undoubtedly a genius in his own right, Christie devoted his energies to the production of high speed AFVs, and his M1931 design was capable of running on either wheels or tracks.

In 1931 the Russians were not inhibited by any of the tactical dogmas finding favour in more traditional Western Armies, and in building up their own Armoured Force they were prepared to accept the best ideas available, whatever their source. They therefore purchased two M1931 type chassis from Christie, and proceeded virtually to copy the design for their projected light medium tank known officially as the Bystrochọdyi (Fast Tank) series.

[Imperial War Museum

BT2 shows its paces

In the BT series, the Christie suspension was faithfully reproduced in all seven marks and was to astonish foreign observers with its resiliance and robustness. In essence it consisted of four large road wheels per side independently attached to pivoting lever arms in the hull side, supported by heavy coil springs, the latter being housed between the inner and outer thickness of the vehicle hull. An argument against this arrangement is that it consumes vital space that could be used within the vehicle, but as regards cross-country performance and speed, this suspension did all that was asked of it.

The final drive system also displayed typical Christie ingenuity. When the vehicle was travelling on tracks, rollers on the rear sprocket engaged alternate lugs on the track, whilst for running on wheels alone, a chain drive passed from the drive sprocket to a second sprocket mounted behind the rearmost road wheel.

[Imperial War Museum

BT5 without tracks

[Imperial War Museum

BT7

When out of use, the tracks were stored along their respective cat-walks, but a prejudice against wheels-only operation developed early in the series' lifetime. Remarkably a steering wheel was used in conjunction with a clutch and brake system for directional control.

At first the BT series was armed with a 37mm gun which was increased to 45mm in the BT5 of 1932 and to 76.2mm on the 1938 BT7. Whilst no criticism can be levelled at the armament of the series, which was adequate by contemporary standards, protection was rapidly becoming obsolete as a result of the increasing power of anti-tank weapons and it was decided that experiments would be carried out to ascertain the best way of preserving the vehicle's best features whilst incorporating a much improved and consequently heavier system of armour protection.

The BT series served in Spain, Manchuria, Finland and the German invasion of 1941. One receives the impression that the vehicle was something of a disappointment tactically. This is understandable as a two-man turret crew, in my opinion, is only capable of functioning efficiently if provided with adequate vision facilities, and these were lacking to a large degree, episcopes being confined to two horn-like projections on the forward turret roof, supplemented by a few direct vision slits.

[Imperial War Museum

BT7 towing a broken down BA armoured car

EXPERIMENTAL VEHICLES LEADING TO DEVELOPMENT OF T34/76 FROM BT SERIES
A20 – A30 – T32

The year 1938 saw the production of the A20, the first attempt to combine a heavier protection factor with the existing fire power and mobility of the BT series.

In the A20 we see the first glimpses of the hull and turret shape to be adopted in T34. The hull overhung the tracks, the hull sides above track level being angled for better shot deflection, whilst a wide T-shaped glacis plate was set at an angle of 60°. The vehicle retained the wheel-and-track capability of the BT series, running on four pairs of road wheels and being powered by the 450bhp engine which achieved a 50mph top speed on wheels.

Maximum armour thickness was 25mm and the vehicle's armament comprised a 45mm gun with a co-axial mg, and a hull mg.

In 1939 the 76.2mm gun already used in the BT7 was mounted in the A20 turret, the vehicle so armed being classified as the A30.

Also in 1939 was produced an alternative solution to the problem, the T32. In this vehicle the number of road wheels was increased to five pairs. The armour was increased to 45mm and the turret fitted with the 76.2mm gun. The same basic shape as A20 was adopted, although the hull was naturally longer. The wheel-and-track feature was dispensed with.

On completion of the T32 prototype, comparative tests were held with the A20 and whilst the latter probably proved the better cross-country vehicle, T32 was preferred in view of the better fire power/protection relationship.

As a direct result of these trials, the design for T34 was established, a design which would have a profound effect on tank designers throughout the world.

T34/76 – MARKS A, B AND C

CREW:	Commander/Gunner, Loader, Driver, Hull Gunner
ARMAMENT:	1 × 76.2mm gun, 2 × 7.62mm mg
WEIGHT:	27 tons 16cwt
LENGTH:	21ft 7in
WIDTH:	9ft 10in
HEIGHT:	8ft 0in
SPEED:	32mph max
ARMOUR:	Glacis 45mm/60°, Turret front 65mm/rounded

At the commencement of Operation Barbarosa the German Army was faced with approximately 22,000 Russian tanks, comprised mainly of T26, BT, T28 and T35 types, all obsolete by German standards and certainly no match for the sophisticated German vehicles and tactics. In consequence, the Wehrmacht wiped the floor with such armoured formations as it encountered and had no reason to suppose that it would not continue to do so.

What is not generally known is that prior to the German invasion, over 1.000 T34s had been completed and the fact that these vehicles were not committed to the shambles occurring in

T34/76 *[Israeli Embassy*

[Israeli Embassy

T34/76A

Western Russia speaks volumes for the self-control of STAVKA. It is possible that it was their intention that the Wehrmacht should blunt itself on the weaker brethren and then be faced by an unknown quality in some quantity. However, students of military history may note with some cynicism that the first mass committal to battle of the T34 occurred at Borodino in October 1941 and reflect upon the circumstances giving rise to the battle at that place in 1812.

Borodino was by no means the first appearance of T34. It had been used earlier in 1941 to support local offensives, but superior German tactics had been able to deal with the vehicle satisfactorily. But from October 1941 onwards, the Russian tactics improved, as did productive capacity, and the "happy time" of the Panzers was at an end. General Guderian, commenting upon the unhappy situation of the German Panzer Troops, has mentioned that in the opinion of those officers most directly concerned with

T34, the vehicle should simply be copied. Other German senior officers were equally unstinting in their praise of the vehicle.

Such praise was well deserved, for in 1941 both German and Western design was behind the Russians by as much as two and three years respectively.

We have already studied the ancestry of the design and noted that it included the Soviet designers' best endeavours to combine fire power, mobility and protection in one vehicle. Let us now examine this remarkable vehicle in detail.

The chassis was of course based upon the Christie suspension system and had five pairs of road wheels. The vehicle was powered by the V2 diesel engine of 12 cylinders including aluminium components, which produced 500bhp at 1800rpm, giving an excellent power to weight ratio of 17.9bhp per ton. The drive sprockets were, of course, at the rear.

Tracks were of the wide (19in) skeleton type and their construction is of particular interest. The track pins, which were round-headed, were inserted from the inside and no retaining device was used on the track itself. Instead, a curved wiper plate

[Imperial War Museum

Captured T34/76A

[Imperial War Museum

T34/76B

was welded to each side of the hull at the rear, at a level with the top run of the track. Therefore, any loose track pin passing the wiper plate in motion was immediately knocked into place.

The hull overhung the tracks and had sloped sides. The glacis plate, set back at an angle of 60°, was 45mm thick, thus giving the same protection as a vertical plate 90mm thick. In the glacis plate were set the driver's hatch containing episcopes and a hull-mounted mg.

The cast turret was extremely cramped and mounted the 1938 Model 76.2mm gun 30.5 calibres long, in addition to a 7.62mm co-axial mg.

In 1942, a newly designed hexagonal turret was mounted on the chassis, the vehicle then being designated T34/76B. The length of the gun was increased to 41.2 calibres yielding a higher muzzle velocity of 2172ft/sec. At the same time, the thickness of the frontal armour was increased to 47mm. In 1943 a further modification was carried out to the turret by the addition of a commander's cupola. In this form the vehicle was known as T34/76C.

Internally, the vehicle was divided into three compartments: driving, fighting and engine. Looking forward, the driver sat on the left behind the usual controls, clutch, brake, accelerator, steering levers and handbrake. To his right sat the hull gunner, who also operated the wireless on those tanks so equipped. An escape hatch was provided for him in the floor in front of his seat. In the turret, the Commander/Gunner was positioned on the left of the gun, the loader on the right. Both worked in extremely cramped conditions. Access to the turret was provided by a clumsy one-piece hatch, so large that the commander's vision was severely curtailed when open. When closed down in Marks A and B, visual aids for the commander were limited to one horn episcope and the gun sights. Main armament ammunition was stowed in bins under the turret floor, although nine rounds were available for immediate use in racks on the walls. A total of 77 main armament rounds was carried in the required proportions of AP, HE and shrapnel.

T34/85

CREW:	Commander, Gunner, Loader, Driver, Hull Gunner
ARMAMENT:	1 × 85mm gun, 2 × 7.62mm mg
WEIGHT:	32 tons
LENGTH:	21ft 7in
WIDTH:	9ft 10in
HEIGHT:	8ft 11in
SPEED:	32mph
ARMOUR:	Glacis 75mm/60°

After the Wehrmacht had overcome its initial shock upon encountering T34/76, it rapidly set about producing solutions to the problem in the form of the long-barrelled Pzkfw Mk IV and Panther. To preserve the lead in gunpower, and also to eliminate as many defects as possible from the T34/76 design turret, a completely new turret was designed mounting the 85mm D-5-5-85 gun 51.5 calibres long, which produced results approximately 60% better than the earlier mark of 76.2mm gun. In addition, the vehicle's crew had been increased to five by the addition of a gunner to the turret crew, with obvious advantages. The commander was provided with a rudimentary cupola, improving his visual aids considerably. Access to the new turret was gained by two small hatches instead of one large one, and some attention was paid to crew comfort by the installation of two mushroom-type ventilators to the right rear of the commander's cupola. Types of ammunition included an APBC AP round, APHE and HE.

[Imperial War Museum

T34/85 in the Balkans

By 1944, the vehicle was in service. It has remained active until the present day in certain areas of the world, being used by the Egyptians in the Yemen, and no doubt the Israeli Army has its share as a result of the Six Day War. In the Red Army T34/85 began to be phased out in 1953 with the introduction of T54, but was still in use during the Hungarian uprising of 1956, and probably disappeared from the service of the European satellites in about 1959. T34/85 was also supplied to Syria, Iraq, Algeria, China and North Korea.

In the Korean war, the T34/85s of the North Korean Army caused such alarm and despondency that the first phase of the war took on the appearance of a Communist Blitzkrieg. However, the arrival of Centurion in the field quickly demonstrated that in medium tank circles T34/85 was strictly *passé*, one account speaking of Centurion absorbing a couple of frantic shots from T34/85, and then literally dismantling its opponent with a first round hit.

In its heyday there can be no doubt that the T34 series was the finest tank design of any army. It has enjoyed the longest service run of any AFV to date, and its qualities of robustness and simplicity ensured maximum operational efficiency from its not very sophisticated crews. Not that it was by any means perfect: Gun depression was limited to 3°, there were constant complaints of transmission failure, and very little attempt at "finish". When, however, one examines the component parts in detail, and relates them to their time of design, one can understand the impact that T34 had on subsequent designs throughout the world.

[Associated Press

T34/85 in Sinai, 1967

T44

CREW:	Commander, Gunner, Loader, Driver
ARMAMENT:	1 × 85mm gun, 1 × co-axial mg
WEIGHT:	32 tons
LENGTH:	21ft 4in
WIDTH:	10ft 9in
HEIGHT:	8ft 2in
SPEED:	32mph
ARMOUR:	Glacis 80mm/60°

The importance of this vehicle is that it provides a direct link between the T34 series and the development of T54. Although it was produced in 1945, it was not manufactured in quantity, and did not replace the T34/85 as the standard medium battle tank of the Red Army.

Basically, T44 was merely an improved version of T34/85. The same 85mm gun was used, and although the turret presented a more streamlined appearance at the front, it suffered from the same overhang at the rear, producing a large shot trap. A flat cupola was provided for the commander.

An improvement on T34/85 was the reduction in height to 8ft 2in. This was achieved by a redesigned hull and chassis. The old Christie-type suspension was abandoned in favour of the torsion bar system. Although still having five pairs of road wheels, T44 presented a larger gap between the first and second pairs, than between the following pairs.

Another interesting feature is the disappearance of the hull mg. Apparently both Russian and British designers had arrived at the same conclusion simultaneously, that the contribution made by the hull gunner could not equal in utility his cubic space when used for ammunition stowage, and although the Russians re-introduced the hull mg in subsequent designs, it became the driver's responsibility.

T54, T55

CREW:	Commander, Gunner, Loader, Driver
ARMAMENT:	1 × 100mm gun, 2 × 7.62mm mg, 1 × 12.7mm mg
WEIGHT:	36 tons
LENGTH:	21ft 0in
WIDTH:	10ft 9in
HEIGHT:	10ft 9in
ARMOUR:	Glacis 85mm/30°, Turret, front and side, 100–105mm, rounded

The need to keep ahead of the West in gun power was accelerated by the Korean war which demonstrated that T34/85 was no longer the paragon it had once been, when faced with up-to-date equipment.

T54 was introduced into service about 1953, and is armed with a 100mm gun 54 calibres long, being the same D-10 SM 1944 model used in the SU100 tank destroyer, producing an AP muzzle velocity of just below 3000ft/sec. The gun is mounted in a well-styled turret, which because of its inverted saucer shape, presents no shot traps.

The early models of T54 did not have a fume extractor fitted to the gun, and in this form the vehicle is known as T54A.

In 1955 the gunnery equipment was improved by the addition of stabilisation gear in elevation only, and by the addition of a fume extractor to the end of the barrel. Depression, however, is limited to 5°. This model is known as T54B.

The chassis was inherited from T44, being of the torsion bar suspension type, with the same basic wheel arrangement, there being a noticeable gap between the first and second pairs of road wheels. In the case of T54, however, the Christie method of engagement between the final drive and the track was replaced by a conventional driving sprocket, mounted at the rear. The engine is the usual Russian V-type diesel engine, producing

520hp, and the steering is geared. Auxiliary fuel tanks are mounted on the rear part of the track guards.

Although T54 shows its ancestry in its simple, robust design, it exhibits a growing sophistication. Many of its features fulfil the requirements of a drive to the West, including provision for the 24-hour battle and the crossing of the various defensive river lines.

The driver is equipped for night driving, and the vehicle can wade across rivers up to 18ft in depth by the erection of a tube on the turret top, directional instructions being given by radio from the river bank.

The turret shows provision for a ventilator fan and a separate hatch is provided for the loader, in addition to the commander's cupola hatch. Horizontal handles are provided for infantry.

Ammunition stowage is estimated at 42 rounds, a reasonable figure, but not good by Western standards. This is improved

[Associated Press

T54 and BTR152; Hungary in 1956

T54s in Czechoslovakia, 1968

[Associated Press

upon in T55, a more advanced version of T54, sometimes known as T54C, which, whilst retaining the same basic main armament and layout, is recognisable by the provision of infra-red searchlights for the commander and gunner.

T54, as well as serving in the armies of the Warsaw Pact, has been issued to Egypt, Syria, Algeria, Afghanistan, China, Cuba and Pakistan. It saw action in the recent Arab-Israeli war, where it was penetrated at surprisingly long ranges by Centurion, and was much in evidence during the Hungarian uprising and the invasion of Czechoslovakia.

As the Soviet Union, in common with other powers, is turning more to the idea of one main battle tank, T54 and T55 are being phased out in favour of T62.

T62

CREW: Commander, Gunner, Loader, Driver
ARMAMENT: 1 × 115mm gun, 1 × 7.62mm co-axial mg,
1 × 12.7mm mg
DIMENSIONS: (*estimated*)
WEIGHT: 37 tons
LENGTH: 23ft 5in
WIDTH: 11ft 2in
HEIGHT: 10ft 2in

T62 represents the culmination of 30 years of medium tank design and development. The vehicle is intended to phase out both the heavy T10 and the medium T54 and T55, and provide a standard main battle tank for the Red Army.

Although the vehicle first appeared in 1963, the Russians are, as always, taciturn, and little information is available.

As the general appearance of the vehicle is very similar to T54, the focus of interest is the 115mm gun, 62 calibres long. This differs from the 100mm gun of the T54 in having a fume extractor mounted two-thirds of the barrel length towards the muzzle, the latter being clean. This gun was probably developed as an answer to the British 105mm gun in use in NATO, and although improvement in AP muzzle velocity must have accrued, there is some doubt as to whether this is yet equivalent to that possessed by the 105mm. Having achieved what was hoped to be the answer, Russian design staff must have been horrified by the appearance of the 120mm gun used in Chieftain.

We must also assume that some progress has been made in providing stabilisation of the gun in line as well as elevation, although the gun once again suffers from the Russian defect of minimal depression. Infra-red aids are provided for the commander, gunner and driver, but as neither optical range finder nor ranging gun are used, shooting must still be below NATO standard.

Although the turret has been redesigned to absorb the recoil of the larger weapon, the basic shape of the T54 turret has been retained in a somewhat elliptical format. Arrangement of armour appears to be excellent, the vehicle presenting a mass of deflection surfaces. As one would expect, T62 combines most of the best, and some of the worst, features of Soviet design.

[RAC Tank Museum

T62, on railway platform, gun traversed rear

CHAPTER 4

Heavy Tanks

T35

CREW:	Commander, 1 × 76.2mm Gunner, 1 × 76.2mm Loader, 2 × 45mm Gunners, 2 × 45mm Loaders, 2 × 76.2mm Machine Gunners, Driver
ARMAMENT:	1 × 7.62mm gun, 2 × 45mm guns, 5 × 7.62mm mg
WEIGHT:	45 tons
SPEED:	20mph
ARMOUR:	45mm maximum
INTRODUCED:	1935

As we have seen in the case of T28, Russian tank designers in the early 1930s were intent upon absorbing the best features of foreign designs into their own vehicles, and having decided that the British Independent of 1926 had much to offer, developed multi-turret vehicles for use according to the tactical usages of the day.

The father of the Russian Heavy Tank family was created in the shape of T35, a monstrous vehicle by contemporary standards, weighing 45 tons and having no less than five turrets, intended for the "breakthrough" role, rather in the manner of World War I tanks.

The hull and chassis of T35 have a strong resemblance to Independent in that the vehicle was carried on a large number of small road wheels, and the hull sides were also protected by side plates. Tracks were steered by the clutch and brake principle, but appear to have been rather narrow for the size and weight of the vehicle. The vehicle used the same V12 petrol engine of 500hp used in T28, based on a German BMW Aircraft Engine, and achieved a top speed of 20mph. The unique feature of T35 was its fighting arrangement. A moderately sized central turret carried the main armament, a 76.2mm gun only 16.5 calibres long together with a co-axial mg. Two slightly smaller turrets, mounted fore and aft of the main turret, and slightly off the vehicle's centre line, mounted first 37mm and then 45mm guns, as well as co-axial mgs, and in addition to this, a further mg turret was mounted in parallel to each of the 45mm gun turrets. The mind begins to boggle at the attempt to control the fighting efficiency of such a vast concourse of weaponry simultaneously, and the vehicle must have been a commander's nightmare. One has every sympathy for the unfortunate troop leader trying not only to command his own tank, but also to control the other tanks in his area of responsibility, especially as the visual aids provided were quite inadequate.

[Imperial War Museum

Captured T35—evidently a breakdown. Tracks have been broken deliberately by crew on the top run, allowing them to roll over front idler, thus immobilising vehicle

However, the T35 is an excellent example of Soviet concentration on hitting power, even at this early stage. The vehicle was fitted for radio, the aerial wrapping round the main turret on brackets about 2ft long. T35 was also rumoured to be capable of being sealed against gas, but it is difficult to attest the veracity of this.

The vehicle saw action in the first Russo-Finnish war, and again in 1941 during the German onslaught, when its poor cross-country performance, badly arranged armour and the low muzzle velocity of its guns made it a monolithic sitting duck for Panzer gunners.

T100

CREW:	Commander, Driver, 1 × 76.2mm Gunner, 1 × 45mm Gunner, 2 × Loaders
ARMAMENT:	1 × 76.2mm gun, 1 × 45mm gun, 3 × 7.62mm mg
WEIGHT:	56–58 tons
ARMOUR:	60mm maximum
ENGINE:	500hp, 12-cylinder petrol

In the spring of 1941, a group of Russian officers were given permission to tour the German tank factories. On being informed that Panzerkampfwagen IV was the heaviest German project in hand, their reaction was somewhat sceptical, as the Red Army had had in its possession a 56-ton tank since 1938.

This vehicle was the T100, and from its chassis design was to come the whole Russian heavy tank family, the derivatives of which are still in service today as missile carriers.

The Spanish Civil War had proved that Russian Armour was not proof against the 37mm anti-tank gun, and an armour requirement was set at 60mm, comparable to the British Matilda. Russian designers were still in favour of the multi-turret concept which had already produced T28 and T35, and it was decided that the main armament should be mounted in a turret amidships

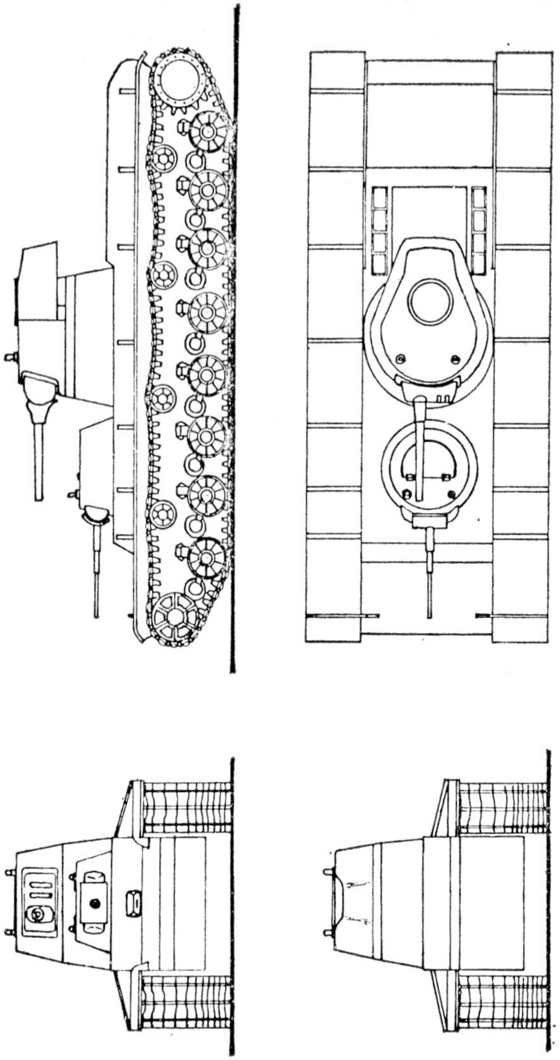

[G. Dooley

T100

on a tall plinth. The style of turret was an adaption of the BT7a turret, and carried a 76.2mm gun and a co-axially mounted mg.

The auxiliary turret was mounted immediately forward of the plinth, and was an adaption of a T35 auxiliary turret, carrying a 45mm gun and a co-axial 7.62mm mg.

The hull was similar to the T35, but a torsion bar suspension was used, from which hung eight pairs of road wheels. The track was carried from the rear drive sprocket to the front idler by four top rollers, and consisted of far wider links than any other track in service on tanks at the time. This development was necessitated by the vehicle's great weight.

Although the T100 design is of considerable interest, in practice the vehicle was a disappointment. By 1939 the exponents of multi-turreted vehicles were losing ground, and the requirement for a single turret mounting a single all-purpose main armament weapon was recognised.

However, the lessons learned in the design and production of T100 were put to good use in its immediate successors, the KV series, which inherited the heavy armour and suspension system.

THE KV SERIES

CREW:	Commander, Gunner, Loader, Driver, Hull Gunner
ARMAMENT:	1 × 76.2mm, 3 × 7.62mm mg
WEIGHT:	43.5 tons
LENGTH:	22ft 0in
WIDTH:	10ft 9in
HEIGHT:	9ft 0in
SPEED:	20–25mph
ARMOUR:	Glacis 75mm, Mantlet 90mm, Hull side 60mm, Turret side 75mm

As well as exposing the many shortcomings of the Soviet Military system, the Russo-Finnish war of 1939, provided the Red Army with an opportunity of testing its replacement for T28 and T35, the Klimenti Voroshilov.

Notwithstanding the vehicle's having been blooded, KV1 still came as an unpleasant surprise to the Wehrmacht. Their answer, in the form of the Tiger, was not available on the Eastern Front until August 1942, and in the interim anti-tank gunners and tank crews were faced with a vehicle of very capable gun power and such a degree of armoured protection that frontal penetration with weapons then available proved most difficult beyond the shortest ranges. However, at this stage of the war, Russian battle practice with regard to armour was still in a rudimentary state of development, and the advantages gained by the vehicle were lost by its users in dissipating its available strength in penny packets which succumbed inevitably to German expertise. Nonetheless, the KV series proved formidable opponents and were the mainstay of Soviet heavy armour until the development of the JS series.

KV Mks 1a, 1b and 1c differed little. The vehicle was carried on six small road wheels per side, utilising the torsion bar method of suspension. The drive sprocket was at the rear, the track being carried forward to the front idler by three top rollers. The road wheels are of interest as they consisted of a layer of rubber between the steel hub and rim, thus providing the cross-country performance of the suspension with a degree of resilience, although shortening track life. Power was provided by the same modification of a V12 water cooled aero engine used in T34, adapted to give slightly more power. Steering was effected by the clutch and brake system.

The layout of the fighting compartment represented a considerable advance on the confusing state of affairs evidenced in T35. Responsibility for this improvement was claimed, modestly, by Stalin himself. Be that as it may, the improvement was such that the vehicle commander was now able to concentrate his energies on one main armament weapon system, which without

[Imperial War Museum

KV1, showing mg mounting in rear of turret

doubt increased the fighting efficiency of the vehicle well beyond that of its multi-turreted ancestors. Again the provision of a separate loader and gunner left the commander's attention freer to attend to other battlefield exigencies. Apart from his obvious function, sitting behind his ball-mounted mg and to the left of the driver, the hull gunner operated the radio on those vehicles fortunate enough to be so equipped.

The main armament consisted of the Model 1939 76.2mm gun, 30.5 calibres long. In due course KV1 came to be equipped with the Model 1940 gun, again of 76.2mm, but 41.5 calibres long, the resulting increase in muzzle velocity improving the armour-piercing performance of the gun.

An odd feature of the KV1 turret was the mg mounted in the rear face of the turret, possibly as a last survival of the multi-turreted "infantry tank" complex.

In general, KV1 showed the first signs of achievement by Russian designers of a workable fire power/protection/mobility relationship, with a bias towards the first two of these essentials. The gun was better than that carried by contemporary tanks, allied or enemy. Armoured protection was exceeded in thickness only by the British Matilda, and the tracks had been broadened to allow for local conditions.

However, the KV1 did have its faults, not least of which was its transmission. Track life tended to be short, and armour was not distributed to its best advantage bearing in mind the weight of the vehicle. From the crews' point of view, major deficiencies were the poor visual arrangements and insufficient access hatches to the vehicle.

The final development of the KV series was the KV85. This vehicle appeared in 1943 as a stop-gap measure neccesitated by increased German gun power, soon to be superseded by the JS series. KV85 was a composite vehicle, consisting of the standard KV chassis upon which was mounted the T34/85 turret and main armament.

[Imperial War Museum

KV85

JSI, II & III

CREW: Commander, Gunner, Loader, Driver
ARMAMENT: 1 × 122mm gun, up to 3 × 7.62mm mg
WEIGHT: 45 tons
LENGTH: 22ft 6in
WIDTH: 10ft 3in

HEIGHT: 9ft 0in (JSIII 8ft 0in)
SPEED: 20–23mph
ARMOUR: 140mm (200mm JSIII) maximum, 30mm min.

The arrival on the Eastern Front of Panther and Tiger convinced STAVKA that the tank battle could no longer be won by T34/85 and the KV series alone. The requirement was therefore for a vehicle capable of carrying a sufficiently large gun to deal with the German heavies.

The choice of weapon fell upon the 122mm gun, which had previously been developed as an artillery piece. Tests showed that the weapon was adequate for the task it had been set, although the gun achieved the destruction of the target by the sheer weight of its projectile rather than by high muzzle velocity or quality of shot. However, the end justified the means, although the employment of such a large weapon naturally required the design of a larger turret than any currently in service, although a large muzzle brake was fitted to the gun.

The shape chosen for the turret of JSI was similar to that employed in KV85, but larger, again having a large cupola to the turret rear.

The hull of the vehicle was a redesigned version of the KV, adapted to carry the new turret well forward. JSI had the same stepped arrangement for the glacis and driver's plates, and incorporated a hull mg, but JSII had a clean rounded glacis and dispensed with this. In the case of both vehicles, the hull now overhung the tracks, both to lower the vehicle height and absorb better the extra weight, and incorporated sloped side armour for greater protection. The whole JS series carried the cylindrical external fuel tanks which were so much a feature of the Russian wartime design. A distinctive feature of JSI and II was the mg found in the rear wall of the turret, inherited from the KV.

Over 2,000 JSI and II were produced by the end of the war, the vehicle being employed as the mainstay of heavy tank companies and regiments. There can be no doubt JSII continued to serve in this capacity for a time after the war's end, both in the Red Army and in the armies of the satellites.

Whilst all JS tanks were carried on an improved KV chassis, JSIII presented a very different appearance to its two predecessors. It is doubtful whether JSIII was in active service before the end of the war, and it may have been the Kremlin's intention as the Eastern Front crumbled into ruin, that the vehicle's debut should have a propaganda and political impact upon its Western allies. If this was the Russian intention, it achieved and deserved considerable success. As the Russian contingent rolled down the Charlottenburg Chaussee in the Berlin Victory Parade of 7th September 1945, British, American and French observers were both impressed and alarmed by the appearance of the new heavy tank.

It was no surprise to see the long 122mm gun. This had been in use in JSI and II, in certain Tank Destroyers, and its efficiency was beyond doubt. Nor was the improved KV chassis a novelty.

What did cause concern was the newly designed turret, the formidable rearrangement of the armour, and the low height and weight of the vehicle in relation to the size of its armament.

[RAC Tank Museum

JSI

[RAC Tank Museum

JSIII

The cast turret was reminiscent in shape of a deep inverted saucer. The glacis was made up of two five-sided plates steeply inclined and meeting in the form of a flat "V". The overall effect was of a mass of deflection angles with no shot traps. Maximum armour protection had been increased to 200mm.

As in the case of JSII the glacis was clean, no provision being made for a hull mg, cubic stowage space being rightly considered of more value than any possible contribution to be made by this weapon. The driver was now seated amidships, immediately behind the junction of the two glacis plates.

However, a heavy 12.7mm mg was mounted on the turret top, and a 7.62mm mg was co-axially mounted with the main armament. Poor provision was made for the commander's optical requirements, as the cupola which appeared in JSII had largely disappeared. In accordance with Russian practice, the turret was fitted with numerous handles for the use of infantry passengers.

The vehicle was powered by a 550bhp engine which produced a speed of 23mph. An interesting feature was the provision of access hatches in the rear wall of the hull to facilitate maintenance.

JSIII was considered to be the world's most powerful tank until approximately 1956. Western designers strove to find an answer to its gun power and protection in larger tanks such as

M103 and Conqueror, and in upgunning existing vehicles such as Centurion with 105mm guns.

For all its formidability, however, JSIII suffered from one serious defect. The streamlined shape and low height of the vehicle had been obtained at the expense of internal space, and ammunition stowage was restricted to 28 main armament rounds. This was far less than the carrying capacity of its Western counterparts, and in terms of the contemporary gunnery techniques meant that JSIII could engage a mere 9 armoured targets without replenishing, assuming all rounds to be AP. The period that the vehicle could remain in action, therefore was strictly limited, and it is therefore fair to assume that its use would have been confined to the set piece breakthrough rather than the encounter battle.

Like its direct ancestors, JSIII served with the Heavy Tank Regiments of the Armoured and Mechanised Divisions. It was issued to the Warsaw Pact allies and the UAR. It has seen action in the Hungarian uprising of 1956, and in the Arab-Israeli war of 1967, and has, therefore found its way into the Israeli hands as a result of the Sinai débacle. Since 1957 JSIII has been replaced by T10.

T10

CREW:	Commander, Gunner, Loader, Driver
ARMAMENT:	1 × 122mm gun, 1 × 12.7mm mg, 1 × 7.62mm mg
WEIGHT:	50 tons
LENGTH:	25ft 2in
WIDTH:	10ft 10in
HEIGHT:	7ft 11in
SPEED:	26mph
ARMOUR:	200mm maximum

Because of the small ammunition stowage capacity and consequent tactical limitations imposed by the JSIII design, attempts were made to remedy those defects early in the 1950s by enlarging the basic hull design of the JS series both in length and width, whilst retaining the same overall shape.

The most obvious external difference between the new T10 design and its predecessors was the addition of one further pair of road wheels. The successful glacis plate design of JSIII was incorporated in the new vehicle and long external stowage boxes were provided along the side of the hull, overhanging the tracks.

The turret was of a similar design to that carried on JSIII but was larger, providing considerably more internal space. A flat cupola was introduced for the commander, with a much improved visual capacity.

The 122mm gun was modified by the inclusion of a fume extractor mounted slightly behind the very prominent muzzle brake. Rate of fire tended to be slow, as in the case of the JS series, because the projectile and propellant had to be loaded separately but the vehicle was able to carry approximately 50% more ammunition than the JSIII.

Having a more powerful version of the same type of diesel engine used in the JS series, the vehicle was able to achieve approximately 26mph, utilising an estimated 700hp.

T10 represents the final stage of development of the well tried, simple and robust design initiated by the KV series. Although the vehicle first appeared in 1957, there is reason to believe that it may have been in service for some time before that. T10 replaced JSIII in the heavy tank regiments, and is known to be still in service, as is evidenced by the newsreels of the events in Prague in 1968.

However, as the Red Army, in common with the armies of other great powers, moves towards the introduction of a main battle tank to replace both the medium and heavy types, T10 is being steadily withdrawn from service.

CHAPTER 5

Self-propelled Guns

Tank Destroyers, Air Portable AFVs, Armoured AA Mountings

ALTHOUGH various forms of self-propelled guns had existed during World War I, it was as a result of the studies carried out by the German General Staff in the inter-war years, that the assault gun sprang into prominence.

The German theory of direct and immediate fire support for the infantry, not only with the HE but also AP weapons, very quickly found favour with the Russians.

The Red Army produced one or two unsuccessful prototypes in the 1930s, but the first production vehicle to be made was a

[Imperial War Museum

Captured KV2 assault howitzer

[Israeli Embassy

SU76

self-propelled howitzer known as KV2, which made its appearance in 1940. This vehicle was a most clumsy affair, consisting of a huge slab-sided turret mounted on a KV chassis. Armament consisted of a 122mm or 152mm howitzer. A ball-mounted machine gun was installed in the rear face of the turret, but the co-axial and hull mg appear to have been dispensed with. Trans-

[Imperial War Museum

SU76 "shooting-in" an infantry attack

mission and steering failures were frequent, due to the vehicle's weight of 52 tons, which was extremely heavy by contemporary standards. The great height of the vehicle, over 11ft, made concealment a difficult task, and consequently it had a short service life.

The next vehicle to appear was the SU76. This derived its title from the Russian *Samachodnya Ustanovka*, meaning literally self-propelled gun, and the type of gun carried, and this formula has been carried on to the present day. The chassis was a lengthened T70 light tank chassis, incorporating an additional pair of road wheels. The fighting compartment was housed at the rear, and mounted a 76.2mm high velocity gun with a muzzle brake and external recuperators. Maximum armour thickness was 35mm. The 6 cylinder petrol engine could produce a speed of 25mph, but as this was less than that of T70, SU76 was relegated to the role of infantry support. The difference in speed can be attributed to the increased weight of the vehicle, which was 2½ tons heavier than T70. Once again, the height of the vehicle made it unsuitable for tank hunting, and its open top was a disadvantage.

SU76 was introduced in 1942, and later in the same year appeared SU122, a short 122mm self-propelled howitzer of some 32 tons weight, mounted on T34 chassis. Like SU76, SU122 had external recuperators. In SU122 we see for the first time the shape which was to become traditional in Russian tank destroyers and self-propelled howitzers, an angled armoured box built onto the front of an existing tank chassis, with a large bulbous mantlet mounted in the front plate, to the right of the vehicle's centre line.

The reasons for the adoption of this shape are interesting. The size of gun which can be mounted on a conventional tank is strictly limited by the diameter of the turret ring because of the problems of retaining the recoil within the space available. If, however, the gun is mounted well forward and is designed to fire only in a limited arc either side of the vehicle's zero line, additional space is available, and consequently a larger gun can be installed than on a tank chassis of the same size. The following example of running mates will illustrate the point:

Tank	*Tank gun*	*SU*	*SU gun*
T34/76	76.2mm	SU85	85mm
T34/85	85mm	SU100	100mm
JS	122mm	JSU152	152mm

Other advantages obtained by adopting this shape include reduced cost of production, lower height than the conventional tank, and increased ammunition stowage capacity.

The disadvantages of the design are, of course, inherent in the limited traverse available for the main armanent, usually only 10° or less either side of zero. To engage a target outside this arc, it is necessary to move the whole vehicle, a difficult operation if it is dug in. Therefore, apart from shooting in major assaults, the role of the SUs was designed for defence in the forward defended localities in close co-operation with the infantry.

Almost concurrent with the introduction of SU122 was that of the SU152 gun howitzer, consisting of a 152mm gun mounted on a KV chassis.

SU85 tank destroyer *[RAC Tank Museum*

The first tank destroyer to achieve continuous success was SU85, utilising the T34 chassis. The vehicle was 7ft 9in high, whilst overall length was 26ft 8in. It weighed 29 tons, and could achieve a speed of 34mph. Armoured protection was 45mm plate welded together, maximum protection for the fighting compartment being at the front, where the plate was angled at 50°. The fighting compartment could stow 48 rounds, consisting of HE, APHE, or APBC in the proportion required for the operation in hand. Although episcopes were provided on a reasonable scale, the commander's cupola was a poor affair. No machine guns were carried.

In cases where the vehicle was fitted for radio, the crew consisted of commander, gunner, loader, operator and driver.

With its D5-5-85 gun, the SU85 was the usual running mate of T34/76. However, when T34/85 appeared on the battlefield, the immediate requirement was for a tank destroyer capable of giving support beyond the AP range of the 85mm gun. This led to the development of the SU100, a vehicle similar in design to SU85, carrying a D10S 100mm gun 54 calibres long. Because of the larger ammunition required for this gun, SU100 carried only 34 rounds.

Improvements upon the SU85 included the installation of a commander's cupola at the right front of the fighting compartment, and the provision of a mushroom ventilator immediately behind this. The vehicle's overall length is 32ft 10in, height is 8ft 4in and weight 32 tons. Armoured protection on the front plate was again a great improvement, being 75mm set at 40°, whilst the large rounded mantlet is 110mm thick. In spite of the additional weight, there was little difference in speed between SU85 and SU100. The vehicle was operated by a crew consisting of commander, gunner, loader and driver. The SU100 was a most successful design and is still in service with the Warsaw Pact Armies, and has also been supplied to the UAR and Iraq. Its greatest fault lies in the very small degree of depression

SU100 tank destroyer [Israeli Embassy

obtainable on the gun, 2° on earlier marks, improved to 4° after the war, which makes the engagement of a target from a reverse slope position a difficult matter without exposing the vehicle.

A contemporary of the SU100 was the JSU122, a tank destroyer based upon the JS chassis, designed for use in conjunction with heavy tanks. Weighing 46 tons, this vehicle was capable of a maximum road speed of 23mph and was 10ft in height. When mounting the 122mm D-25-5 gun, 43 calibres long, overall length was 33ft 5in. When mounting the A19S, 45 calibres long, with muzzle brake, overall length was reduced to 32 ft. An estimated 40 rounds could be stowed.

Although presenting a more slab-sided appearance than SU85 or SU100, JS122 was well armoured, having 122mm at 60° in the

JSU122 tank destroyer [Imperial War Museum

front plate whilst the huge mantlet was rounded and 200mm thick. A ventilator was positioned in the roof of the fighting compartment, and whilst the commander was not provided with a cupola, his hatch was split to open sideways, whereas the commanders' hatches in SU85 and SU100 were one piece affairs, opening to the front, and this impeded vision unless the commander was prepared to expose himself.

The commander of JSU122 was equipped with a 12.7mm heavy mg. The vehicle carried the usual crew of 4/5 depending on whether a radio was fitted. The vehicle was usually employed in the tank destroyer company of the heavy tank regiments. An adaption of the vehicle carrying a 29 calibre 152mm gun howitzer was known as JSU152.

The development of T54, T10 and T62 tended to make tank destroyers of the type of SU100 and JSU152 obsolete, and tank destroyers in service today are of the air portable types.

The first Russian air portable tank destroyer appeared in 1957 under the title ASU57. This vehicle is basically an open-topped armoured box on a small tracked chassis with a front drive sprocket, three road wheels suspended by torsion bars and two top rollers. It is only 4ft 8in high, and overall length 12ft 2in. It is estimated that the vehicle weighs 6 tons. The gun is a 57mm piece, and it is possible that it can be removed through doors at

[Israeli Embassy

JSU122a tank destroyer

JSU152 assault howitzer [Imperial War Museum

the vehicle's rear for installation on a ground mounting, thus releasing the carriage for other duties. The 120hp engine is situated at the front. The crew consists of one driver plus four crewmen for the gun, and it therefore appears unlikely that anything other than immediate requirement rounds are stored on board, the remainder being picked up on arrival in the dropping zone. Maximum armoured protection is estimated at 12mm, and although the machine is undoubtedly ingenious, it must be conceded that it is highly vulnerable to anything heavier than small arms fire.

The latest development in the airborne tank destroyer is the ASU85. This vehicle appeared in 1961, and is based upon the useful PT chassis. The armament consists of an 85mm gun, with fume extractor and muzzle brake, mounted centrally in the high sloping front plate of the fighting compartment, which, following tradition, is itself mounted at the front of the vehicle. The fighting compartment is a well angled structure with the usual flat top. Two large drum tanks are mounted on the rear plate of the high engine compartment. A prominent feature is the provision of infra-red aids for night shooting. Vehicle dimensions are:

[*Universal Press International*

ASU85 airborne tank destroyer in the fiftieth Anniversary of Revolution Parade in Red Square

height, 6ft 2in; overall length, 28ft 4in; width, 10ft 2in; weight, 18/20 tons; speed (est), 25mph.

Unlike its ancestors, it is believed that ASU85 is confined to the anti-tank role, and is not required to give direct support with HE shells.

In 1957, the Red Army produced a most effective anti-aircraft tank, to be known as ZSU57-2. This consisted of the same hull and engine as employed in T54, whilst the number of road wheels was reduced to four pairs and mounted an opentopped, box-shaped turret containing twin 57mm S60 anti-aircraft guns. These guns have the exceptional length of 73 calibres, and are fitted with multi-hole muzzle brakes, and are also equipped with radar control. The very high muzzle velocity obtained renders the vehicle suitable also for employment against hard ground targets if necessary. Armoured protection is estimated at 80mm.

ZSU57-2 is crewed as follows: commander, 2 × gunners, 2 × loaders, driver. It weighs 35 tons, is 20ft 4in long, 7ft 10in high and 10ft 11in wide. A maximum speed of 30mph is obtainable.

A recent Soviet production is a further anti-aircraft tank based upon the PT chassis. This is the ZSU-23-4. A flat box-like turret mounts a circular radar scanner at the rear, controlling the four 23mm cannon housed in a recessed mantlet in the turret front. There is a commander's cupola forward and to the left of the scanner, and a gunner's hatch to the right, in parallel. The driver's vision block can be protected by dropping a hinged slotted visor. It is possible that provision has been made for infra-red aids for night driving.

Informed sources quote the vehicle's dimensions as being: length, 20ft; height, 8ft 6in exclusive of scanner; width, 9ft; weight, 15 tons.

A crew of three is carried.

In most Western armies, self-propelled guns are the responsibility of the Artillery, but in the Red Army they are manned by

[Associated Press

ZSU57-2 anti-aircraft tanks; May Day, 1963

armoured troops and form an integral part of a formation, co-operation between tank crews and self-propelled gunners having been brought to a fine art by long practice. There is much to be said in favour of the Russian school of thought.

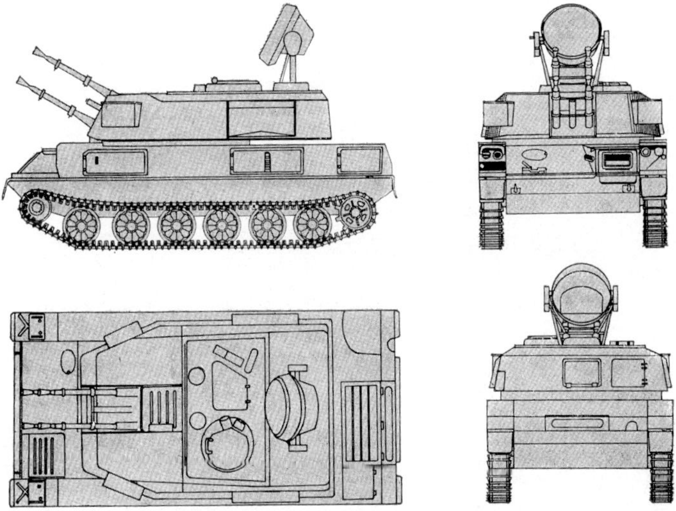

[German Recognition Manual

ZSU23-4 anti-aircraft tank

CHAPTER 6

Armoured Personnel Carriers

Scout Cars, Supply Carriers

ARMOURED BATTLES are not won by tanks alone. Unless full co-operation exists between all the teeth arms of an army, any large scale operation risks failure. We have seen in the previous chapter how self-propelled howitzers and tank destroyers were designed to provide an artillery element within the structure of a mechanised force. Let us now examine the vehicles supplied to the infantry of the Red Army to enable them to keep up with their tanks and secure the ground already won.

The first instance of troops being lifted into battle by armoured vehicles occurred in the allied offensives of 1918, when machine gun teams were carried forward across newly won ground, and dropped off to form the first element of a defensive crust against a counter-attack.

After the end of World War I, these simple experiments seem to have been forgotten for nearly twenty years. However, in its conception of Blitzkrieg, the German General Staff realised the necessity of providing the infantry of the Panzer division with a means of keeping up with their tanks, and produced a series of excellent half-tracked vehicles which were capable of many other roles in addition to carrying infantry. The Western allies also produced armoured personnel carriers in the form of the American M3 half-track and the fully tracked Kangaroo, the latter being basically a turretless tank, but the poor Russian mechanised infantryman of the time was still being bounced around the battlefield in unarmoured lorries, with the attendant

[Associated Press

BTR40 APC/SC in Prague, 1968

consequences of a comparative reduction in mobility and increase in vulnerability.

The story of the Russian APC does not properly begin until after the war when Soviet designers had had an opportunity to examine the existing contemporary models.

1946 saw the introduction of BTR40, a small four-wheeled vehicle with an open-topped box-like rear compartment capable of carrying a section of infantry, modelled on the earlier American White Scout cars. The vehicle was fitted with four-wheel-drive, but remained basically an armoured truck. Apart from the personal arms of the occupants, no provision was made for the carrying of armament, nor was it possible to fight from within the vehicle without exposing oneself. Protective armour was sufficient to keep out small arms fire only, and if fired into from above the vehicle must have been a death trap. In consequence, it was employed mainly on reconnaissance and liaison duties.

Introduced in the same year, the BTR152 was a better design, although having many of the same faults. Resembling a wheeled version of the M3 half-track, the vehicle was driven on all six wheels, and in addition to its own crew of three could carry 12 infantrymen. Whilst again resembling an open box, the sides of the vehicle were angled at the corners to provide deflection surfaces and three ports per side were provided for fighting from within the vehicle. Egress for the occupants was either by jumping over the side or by a door in the rear wall. A heavy machine gun of either 12.7mm or 14.5 mm was mounted on the rear of the driving compartment. Later versions of the vehicle introduced a central tyre pressure control system, enabling the driver to alter the tyre pressure to suit the going. Some versions were also fitted with an armoured roof, but this was by no means general.

BTR152, whilst high, has a good cross-country performance, and is suited for mass production, spares being interchangeable with the SK57 truck. It remains in service today, and in addition to its APC role can be used as a towing vehicle for artillery and heavy mortars, as a command vehicle, mortar carrier, or in the anti-aircraft role.

[Associated Press

BTR152 burned out in Gaza Strip, 1967

In 1958 a tracked APC was introduced into the armoured reconnaissance units. This vehicle is designated BTR50(P) and is fully amphibious, being based upon the PT76 chassis, using the same water propulsion units, and is therefore more manoeuvrable in the water than its Western counterparts. The turret of PT76 has been replaced by an open box with a capacity for 12 infantrymen in rather crowded conditions. A commander's cupola is fitted at the left front corner of the superstructure, with the one piece hatch opening forwards. No provision has been made for fighting from within the vehicle, although a 12.7mm mg can be installed behind the commander's cupola. Egress is over the side.

A further amphibian APC appeared in 1960. This is the eight-wheeled BTR60(P) and it is envisaged that it will replace BTR152 in due course. Each of the eight wheels is driven, and is independently suspended. The open topped hull resembles a punt with sides angled inwards, a shallow glacis and backward-sloping rear decking. The hull sides show provision for weapon ports and half doors. BTR60(P) is heavily armed for an APC, carrying 1 × 12.7mm mg and 3 × 7.62mm mg, although the

[*Associated Press*

BTR60(P) APCs in May Day Parade, 1963

[Associated Press

BRDM with Sagger missile

latter can be unshipped if necessary for use in ground mountings. It is fitted with a water jet propulsion unit, and its performance in the water is good enough for it to have been issued to Marine units as well as the Army. In addition to its crew of three, a section of nine infantrymen can be carried.

Another amphibian is the replacement for RTR40, the BRDM scout car. This appeared first in 1959, the earlier versions having the engine at the front, although in later developments this has been moved to the rear. In each case the hull is boat-shaped, whilst the superstructure is similar to that of the British Ferret Mk. I. A crew of three is carried. In the water, the vehicle is propelled by a water jet unit mounted at the rear of the vehicle and movement across difficult country can be assisted by lowering four small retractable wheels suspended between the main road wheels amidships. Later models of BRDM are equipped to carry three guided anti-tank missiles.

A new armoured personnel carrier, designated M1967, appeared in the parade in Red Square held in November 1967 to celebrate the Fiftieth Anniversary of the Revolution. In lay-out, this is comparable to the German APC12-3 (HS30). The vehicle carries a crew of three, plus a section of Infantry who sit "back-to-back" at the rear of the vehicle. The Infantry can close down their compartment by shutting two long hatches which fold together along the vehicle's centre line. Exit from the vehicle is made by two doors mounted in the rear face of the hull. The chassis of the vehicle is similar to the PT series chassis. M1967 carries a gun which, it is believed, is capable of giving HE support and also carries one Sagger anti-tank missile, mounted directly upon the gun. Both the gun and the missile are controlled from a small one-man turret mounted amidships. An interesting feature of the hull design is that not only are there ports for fighting from within the infantry compartment but also each Infantryman has an episcope to provide him with a view of the prevailing tactical situation. This vehicle is undoubtedly one of

SUMMARY OF APCs, SCOUT CARS AND CARRIERS

VEHICLE	TYPE	HEIGHT	LENGTH	WIDTH	WEIGHT	SPEED	ARMAMENT	REMARKS
BTR40	APC/SC	5ft 11in	16ft 5in	6ft 11in	5.3 tons	50mph	—	Wheeled
BTR152	APC	7ft 0in	22ft 10in	7ft 8in	9 tons	43mph	12.7mm or 14.5mm mg	Wheeled
BTR50(P)	APC	6ft 7in	22ft 0in	10ft 1in	15 tons	31mph	12.7mm or 14.5mm mg	Amphibian—tracked
BTR60(P)	APC	8ft 6in	22ft 9in	8ft 6in	—	—	1 × 12.7mm mg 3 × 7.62mm mg	Amphibian—wheeled
BRDM	SC	5ft 10in	16ft 5in	6ft 11in	6 tons	55mph	Guided A/TK missiles occasionally	Amphibian—wheeled
AT-P	Cargo VEH	5ft 7in	13ft 1in	—	6 tons	—	1 × 7.62mm mg	Air portable, tracked. Probably amphibious: capacity ½ ton
GAS47	Cargo VEH	—	—	—	—	—	None	Tracked amphibian: capacity 1 ton
K61	Cargo VEH	—	—	—	—	—	None	Tracked amphibian: capacity 3 tons

the most sophisticated APC's in service today and is extremely heavily armed for its role. It is believed that it will phase out BTR50 in the motor infantry regiments of the armoured divisions.

The solutions to the logistic problems of supporting any amphibious operation had, until World War II, hinged upon the availability of bridges or ferry space. If logistic support for the assault troops can be made independent of bridges and ferries, the assault itself can be delivered with almost as much force as if it were a normal attack, whilst consolidation of a bridge-head can be hastened by the rapid delivery of heavy stores forward. During the latter end of the war, the Western Allies possessed a very adequate sufficiency of amphibious cargo carriers but the Red Army did not possess any such luxury. The matter was not treated as urgent by the Russians and it was not until 1957 that the first purely cargo amphibians were produced.

These were the BAW, which was an almost exact copy of the DUKW, and the K61, which is very similar but which is carried on a tracked chassis with seven pairs of road wheels. Another amphibious vehicle, GAS47, is scarcely armoured and resembles a conventional truck body on a tracked chassis. The load capacity of this vehicle is one ton.

About the same time, an air portable supply carrier known as the AT-P was produced, based upon an enlarged version of the ASU57 chassis. This is manned by a crew of three and can move approximately ½ton of stores. It mounts a 7.62mm mg; the 12mm armoured protection is confined to the crew's compartment.

CHAPTER 7

Special Purpose Vehicles

Armoured Recovery Vehicles, Flamethrowers, Minesweepers, Bridging Tanks, Missile Carriers

An armoured vehicle can be put out of action for a variety of reasons. It can bog down, its automotive components can become casualties to enemy action, or its crew can be killed. In any event, it is desirable that the vehicle should be salvaged from the battlefield to fight another day.

This task can usually be undertaken by the average gun tank, but this represents a squandering of resources and it is obviously preferable to use a vehicle designed exclusively for the purpose, which is capable not only of the physical task of recovery but which is also sufficiently protected to enter the battle zone whilst fighting is still taking place.

To the Russians, an adaption of the SU series was the obvious and logical answer. The vehicle, usually an SU100, is stripped of its main armament and simply equipped with twin heavy duty towing hawsers. This represents a crude solution by Western standards but it must be remembered that since 1942, the Red Army has generally remained in possession of the battlefield after the event and has, in consequence, been able to recover its casualties at leisure. It is fair to say that its recovery teams have never had to work under the same pressures as existed for both sides in the North African Campaign or in Normandy, where recovery of every available vehicle was of prime importance vis-à-vis the next engagement and it is probably anticipated by the Red Army that this facility will continue to be enjoyed in any future conflict. However, recent years have shown the adaption of the T54 and JS chassis to the recovery role, complete with ground spades, winches and other impedimenta.

In launching an armoured assault against prepared positions, many difficulties, in addition to the enemy's fire, must be surmounted. The position may be defended by a minefield and may be fronted by an anti-tank ditch or small stream and will probably contain some defence works which are capable of absorbing any amount of direct shellfire. These tasks fall beyond the capacity of normal gun tanks and are the province of a specially-designed family of vehicles known in armoured circles as "Funnies".

For mine clearing tasks, the Russians adopted the usual system of pushing rollers ahead of the vehicle, exploding mines in its path by the sheer pressure exerted on the ground. The system was first adopted for use on T34 and in this form, twin rollers merely cleared a path in front of the vehicles' tracks, leaving the area between unswept, and is still in use today, T54 having been adapted for the role. An advantage of this type of mine clearing device is that the main armament can still be utilised to the full in the vehicle to which it is fitted.

For bridgelaying vehicles the Red Army has used both the T34 and T54 chassis. Bridges can be of the rigid type, attached permanently to the vehicle, which is driven bodily into the space to be bridged and abandoned until required elsewhere, or of the hydraulic type, in which the bridge pivots over rollers at the front of the vehicle, on to the far bank, when it is dropped, leaving the vehicle itself free for other tasks. A later development was the scissors type of bridge, carried folded in two halves on the vehicle's back, giving a longer reach. Once down, the conventional armour can cross the bridge with the minimum of delay and proceed with the attack. For obvious reasons, bridgelayers are prime

[Universal Press International

Ganef missile carriers

targets and their operations, where possible, are concealed by darkness or smoke.

Another vehicle with a combat engineer role is the Tankdozer. This consists of a dozer blade, fitted to the front of a conventional T34/85 or T54 gun tank, actuated by hydraulic rams. This vehicle can assist operations in a variety of ways, clearing obstructions, moving earth in bulk to provide cover for a consolidation of gains made, or simply filling in craters on vital routes.

A more sinister weapon is the flamethrower tank, designed specifically for use against the obstinate strongpoint, pillbox or bunker. In this field, the Russians received much technical advice from Britain during World War II and fitted a British-type system to T34. The muzzle of the flamethrower was mounted in place of the hull mg, but instead of towing a fuel trailer, the Russians preferred the addition of an extra tank to the rear of the vehicle. The range of the jet was approximately 100 yards.

Whilst Russian special purpose vehicles are no doubt adequate for their respective tasks, the only sector of this field in which there is a lead over the West is that of missile carriers. A series of ingenious adaptions of the chassis of existing tanks has given the Red Army the most mobile tactical missile force in the world, the following types being introduced about 1957.

The PT76 chassis has been used as the basis for the BB-1 missile launcher. The missile has a range of 16 miles and is housed on a launching ramp mounted on the rear of the vehicle, with a securing clamp, locking round the warhead, fixed to the vehicle's front. With the clamp removed, the missile can be traversed and elevated.

The 30-mile range BB-2 rocket is carried on a JS missile launcher Type A which is, as its name implies, an adaption of the JS chassis, with the crew's quarters situated in a large cab at the front of the vehicle. The missile itself is housed inside a cylindrical propellant warmer which forms an integral part of the launching ramp and the protruding warhead is protected by a removable cage. The missile is elevated by means of hydraulic arms. It is not guided.

The same basic adaption of the JS chassis is used in the JS missile launcher Type B, carrying the BB-3 guided missile, which has a range of 60 miles. The missile is raised by hydraulic arms to its firing position on to a ramp carried on a pivot at the rear of the vehicle. Whilst travelling, the missile is protected by a cage.

A lengthened and strengthened JS chassis, with a front drive sprocket, was also introduced in 1957 as a vehicle for a short series of experimental types utilising the ram-jet principle for the firing of long range missiles, but this development was overtaken by others in the guided missile field and abandoned.

The second generation of portable missiles began to appear in

[Associated Press

Scamp missile on JS-type chassis

[Associated Press

Scrooge missile on JS-type chassis

1964 with the Ganef missile, mounted in pairs on a similar chassis to the M1967 Armoured Personnel Carrier. These missiles are mounted with the left-hand missile slightly below the right, to allow adequate clearance of the tail fins on discharge. The range of the rocket is believed to be in the region of 100 miles.

A further development of the JS series of missile carriers carries the Scamp missile, which came into service in 1965. Scamp has the role of an intermediate range strategic missile and is believed to be capable of hitting targets 900 miles away.

A similar JS chassis carries the giant Scrooge ICBM rocket which, it is understood, can operate up to ranges of 3,000 miles.

Naturally, the carriers for Scamp and Scrooge are not intended as launching vehicles for these missiles but it is interesting to note that such a degree of portability exists for such strategic weapons.

[Associated Press

AA missiles on M1967 chassis

CHAPTER 8

Gunnery

A TANK EXISTS solely for the purpose of bringing its gun within killing range of a target. However good the automotive components of a vehicle, or however well arranged its armoured protection, these advantages count for nothing if the gun is unable to fulfil its primary role, that of the destruction of other tanks, at ranges equal to or beyond the capacity of these tanks.

[Imperial War Museum

Breach and fire control equipment of KV1

The gun therefore, provides the starting point for any tank design, and will affect the general shape and size of the vehicle for the simple reason that the recoil of the weapon must be contained within the turret, and therefore the diameter of the turret ring must be tailored to the gun and not vice-versa. Again, the higher the muzzle velocity demanded of the gun for its armour-defeating role, the greater will be the recoil. The problem seems to be of a spiral nature, but an upper limit is reached when the ultimate range of the gun exceeds the vehicle commander's visual ability to locate a target, ie when the target is so far away it cannot be seen, bad weather and concealment factors aside.

Various methods have been employed to contain the recoil. The SU series of SP guns and tank destroyers dispensed with a conventional turret and mounted their guns in an armoured box at the front of the vehicle, thus providing extra space, but at the expense of a severely curtailed traversing capacity. Another method is the fitting of a muzzle brake to the end of the barrel, thus providing an earlier release of pressure with a minimal drop in muzzle velocity.

A considerable amount of the recoil forces are transferred via the trunnions to the vehicle chassis, but some assistance is rendered by the hydraulic recuperator cylinders, whose proper function of course, is to run out the gun at the termination of the recoil.

When firing AP or HE rounds the gun recoils sufficiently for the breech to be tripped into an open position on the run-out, the spent case being ejected by its own inertia at the final point of recoil. Rounds with a lower muzzle velocity give less recoil, and the recoil distance obtained is insufficient to trip the breech block, this having to be operated manually for the next round.

When a vehicle was closed down with the main armament in action, the atmosphere in the turret rapidly became foul from cordite fumes, causing discomfort to the crew and inducing exhaustion on the part of the loader. This has now been remedied to a certain extent by the provision of fume extractors on the barrel of the gun, which operate on a simple vacuum principle, and prevent most of the waste gases trickling back through the breech.

Gun control equipment, in its simplest form, consists of controls for the elevation, depression and traversing of the gun to obtain a lay onto a target at a chosen range, using the graticule pattern on the sight picture of the telescopic sight to verify for elevation and line.

Whilst elevation and depression are put on the gun by hand, traverse has been power-assisted for many years except in the smallest turrets, the final line corrections again being put on by hand. In the matter of stabilisation, the Red Army was behind the West for a number of years, and at first succeeded in achieving a lay stabilised in elevation alone, although it is now believed that full stabilisation has been attained.

Two factors in design put Red Army tank gunners at a dis-

[Imperial War Museum

Rear face of turret, KV1

advantage compared with their Western equivalents. The first results from the adoption of the inverted saucer shape for turrets. Whilst this shape is tactically desirable, it permits only a few degrees of depression, as the upward movement of the breech block in a depressed lay with a minimum of headroom over it, must be limited unless it is to go through the roof on recoil. It is desirable that tanks should engage their opponents from a hull down position but if the target to be engaged lies below the level of the maximum depression obtainable, it becomes necessary to expose the whole vehicle, thus wasting time and nullifying efforts to use ground for concealment and protection, as well as placing the vehicle in a more vulnerable situation.

The second factor is the absence of sophistication in target acquisition. Whilst Western Armies use split image range finders or ballistically matched ranging guns to obtain a first round hit, the Russians seem content to stick to their World War II practice of bracketing the target using graticule pattern corrections based on observing the fall of shot and obtaining a second or third round hit. This method wastes both time and ammunition and, as we have seen, Russian tanks carry less of the latter than NATO vehicles, they are at a disadvantage in a pure slogging match.

Types of ammunition carried include AP rounds of the APBC and HVAP type, an APHE round and a High Explosive round. The first type is employed against purely armoured hard targets where penetration is the prime necessity. This is heavier than the equivalent NATO APDS round, is fired at a lower muzzle velocity and does not achieve the same success. The APHE round can be used against armour up to a medium range but is primarily designed for use against targets where an explosive is required after penetration, for example, buildings or bunkers. The conventional High Explosive shell is of course for use against soft targets or immediate close support for infantry.

Historically, it is interesting to note that no Russian tank has ever been outgunned by a contemporary at the date of its introduction, until the last few years. This was not the result of an inherent Russian technical superiority in the ballistics field as the same facilities existed in Germany in the West, but were simply not applied to tank design until much later; it was a result of common sense.

It is elementary that the longer the gun, the higher the muzzle velocity obtained and the higher the muzzle velocity, the greater the armour defeating capability of the round fired from that gun. Hence the constant increase in gun length already described in this survey.

Perhaps not quite so obvious is the second factor. A large calibre round travelling at the same speed as a small calibre round has greater penetrative power. This principle was used in adapting what was basically an artillery weapon to the JS series.

Comparison of historically contemporary equivalents to Russian tanks will reveal that they were inferior in one or both of these qualities.

[Imperial War Museum

The 122mm gun of JSIII on display

It is to be wondered that until T62, the Red Army did not produce a barrel capable of standing up to the enormous pressures required to achieve the high muzzle velocities attained by Western tank guns since the 105mm was adopted by NATO and even if the gun carried by T62 is as good as the 105mm, which would be surprising, the 120mm gun carried by Chieftain is, without doubt, its peer.

It appears, therefore, that for the first time in its history, the Red Army is behind on gun technology, not only in the physical sense, but also in matters of gun control and target acquisition.

CHAPTER 9

Tactics and Training

IT IS FAIR to say that the tactics adopted for any specific engagement are the product of, firstly, the material available, and secondly the quality as battle practitioners of the soldiers who are to use that material. In the armoured battle, this is especially so, and the two factors interact as nowhere else on the battlefield; a good vehicle is wasted upon an untrained crew, and a well trained crew are unable to give their best in a poor vehicle.

As we have seen, Soviet designs combined robustness with simplicity, both qualities which enabled the training depots and schools to produce large numbers of drivers, gunners and loaders very quickly. As the vehicles lacked sophistication, there was thus less for trainees to learn.

We have also seen how the various branches of the Soviet Armoured Corps have developed over the years, and have studied in detail the manner in which Russian designers have attempted to satisfy the three basic requirements of any armoured fighting vehicle—fire power, mobility and protection. As movement is essential to the armoured battle, a fourth requirement appears immediately—flexibility. This can be defined as the ability to transmit and to receive orders relating to the conduct of the engagement, in other words, the exercise of control and command. Unless flexibility is exercised, the other basic virtues of any armoured fighting vehicle are wasted.

In practice, flexibility is exercised through the radio, and it was in this specific context that the Red Army was most deficient during the 1930s and the war years. Although radios were fitted to Red Army vehicles long before the outbreak of World War II, great problems existed both in the industrial capacity to produce the large number of sets required by the Army, and in the training of an equivalent number of operators to work them efficiently. In consequence, the highly flexible thrusts of the German Panzer Armies in 1941 almost led to the destruction of the numerically superior, but lumbering, mass of Soviet armour, which was simply not equipped either physically or mentally for an onslaught of such mobility.

[Associated Press

A T54 burning in Prague

With the aid of many thousands of British and Canadian W/S 19 sets, the balance was partially corrected, although the scale of issue did not provide for the allotment of one single radio below the level of company commander, except in the most exceptional circumstances. This meant that whilst the Regimental Commander could control his Company Commanders, they in turn could not control the platoon leaders properly. The latter, in fact, probably spent far too long watching the Company Commander's vehicle for hand signals.

This probably explains why, during the war, Soviet armour showed up best in the massive set piece attack rather than in the long range penetration role. It is interesting to note that the average German blitzkrieg advance was 250/300 miles in 2/3 weeks, whilst the best that the Russians could do was 125/150 miles in 3/4½ weeks, except for the Vistula/Oder advance of 250 in just over 3 weeks, and the Manchurian offensive against the Japanese.

Let us now examine the typical Red Army set-piece attack of World War II. In the first instance the medium and heavy artillery, accompanied by the Katyusha rocket batteries, would soften the enemy front with a bombardment of varying duration. Next SU self-propelled guns and tank destroyers would take up position as near as possible to the start line to shoot in the attack and destroy opportunity targets. The attack would then go in three waves.

The first wave, consisting of KV or JS tanks, had the task of neutralising specific targets within the enemy's forward defended locality, such as anti-tank guns, bunkers and strongpoints.

The second wave, consisting of T34s, accompanied by infantry, passed through the first, completed a breach in the enemy's defended area, and then mopped up survivors.

The role of the third wave, again of T34s, was to pass through the first and second and exploit the breach by passing on beyond it, with infantry, to a predetermined objective.

The attack then halted and the new front was stiffened by the arrival of the SUs who had now been released from their support role.

This represents the Red Steamroller at its best. As the attack had been rehearsed thoroughly, commanders and troops at every level knew what to do, where to go and what to expect. In consequence, the attack stood every chance of success. From the enemy's viewpoint it must have been a frightful experience.

However, three things are apparent from this oft-repeated formula. The first is the tremendous concentration of force used to obtain what was in essence a tactical objective. Second, the reliance upon rehearsals tends to make troops less adaptable when not under immediate control in the face of the unexpected event, such as a strong armoured counter-attack, although it must be conceded that the absence of a complete communications net made rehearsals inevitable. Finally, the unwillingness of senior commanders to exploit the situation beyond their allotted objectives when this might have reaped great rewards.

Whilst Red Army strategy cannot be said to have been exactly dashing in the offensive, in defence it was sound. Where the front was threatened, armoured formations were grouped in the rear of the threatened sector ready to put in the counter-attack. When the position was stabilised after the enemy attack had been halted, these formations were committed against the flanks of any salient formed.

At the tactical level tanks were dug in amongst the infantry in well-sighted positions, and camouflaged. In this position, they acted as armoured anti-tank guns or machine gun posts. Tanks were allocated precise areas of responsibility with interlocking arcs of fire. If their infantry were forced to withdraw, the tanks covered them, and then withdrew themselves, leap-frogging by the usual method of fire and movement. If possible, withdrawals were made at night. Naturally, the Russian climate presents certain problems to the pursuit of armoured warfare which do not exist elsewhere. Extremely low temperatures and thick snow in winter, and deep mud during the spring thaws, inhibit large-scale armoured movement for much of the year, but the Russians did not permit these factors to paralyse them completely.

Wide skeleton tracks were provided for driving in snow, and when moving across unknown ground each tank was provided with an escort of four or five skiers who carried out ground reconnaissance ahead of the vehicle. In certain instances tanks have towed armoured sledges, each containing a section of infantry, into an assault, with the twin objects of reducing infantry casualties whilst increasing their mobility.

[Associated Press

A JSIII shattered in Budapest. The turret had been blown 20-25 yards

If in defensive positions or in reserve, tank crews were fortunate in being able to make themselves relatively comfortable. Tanks were covered with snow up to their roofs, to provide a layer of insulation as well as camouflage, and a stove was installed. Engines were started several times during the day and night. Such a snug arrangement must have been envied by their infantry comrades.

Although not provided with night-fighting aids during World War II, tanks and self-propelled guns nevertheless operated at night. After the infantry had infiltrated a position by day, they located suitable targets for the armour, and after establishing contact after last light, guided them into their objective. Close liaison between the two arms was maintained at all times. Generally, the tanks advanced in echelon to achieve deception concerning their exact numbers. Anyone who has worked amongst

[Imperial War Museum

"Tank Marines" mount KVI (left) and T34/76A (right), under fire, in some haste

[Imperial War Museum

T34s at speed, close up to their own barrage

armour at night will understand what a frightening business this is, as it is almost impossible to pinpoint the position of one single tank by its engine noise, and will agree that the sound of many tanks, operating in echelon, can give the impression that one has been completely overrun.

After the tanks and SUs had destroyed their targets, reinforcement infantry occupied the position and established a hard defensive perimeter. Following this, the armour withdrew.

Before examining the tactics which the Red Army may well use if hostilities actually broke out with the West, it is necessary to take a look at the background in which the Red Army officer has to work and make his decisions, as this will acutely affect the conduct of operations.

There is no doubt that the Russian officer is intelligent, capable and professional. He is also a dedicated Communist. His training is thorough and he attends courses regularly to keep himself up to date. He is paid above the level of his civilian counterparts in the professional classes, and his shoulder boards give him a status in society akin to that of officers in the old Imperial Army. He is in every sense a privileged citizen, and occupies a superior grade of accommodation. He has access to consumer goods which are not available to the general public, at subsidised prices. When he retires, he does so on a generous pension. His conduct as an officer and a gentleman can be the subject, if necessary, of a trial by his brother officers at a Court of Honour, another reminiscence of Imperial days.

And yet for all this, he tends to be a solitary being. It is the intention of the rulers of Russia that the Army should be the servant of the Communist Party. Therefore the government installs its Commissars at all levels except the lowest tactical units, to provide political education for the soldiers and to see that the unit continues to follow the party line. The Commissars will also supply reports upon the officers and others within the unit. In addition, specially planted officers, NCOs and soldiers will supply secret reports on their colleagues. The officer therefore finds himself under surveillance both from above and below, and is understandably reluctant to confide in his brother officers on political or professional matters. A further incentive to discretion is the sight of officers considered "unsuitable" finding themselves unemployable in civilian life save as unskilled labourers.

In this atmosphere it is perhaps understandable that senior commanders should blame their subordinates for mishaps in order to keep their own records clean, but the obvious effect of this is the stifling of initiative, as junior commanders will simply not act without direct orders from above. As the armoured battle requires a quick assessment of a situation, followed by swift independent thought and immediate action, this state of affairs is scarcely ideal, and must result in a slow moving battle, lost opportunities, and possible failure.

[Imperial War Museum

Standardisation in all things. T35 main armament and auxiliary turrets in use on armoured train. Note the Commissar standing between the train commander and the crew

The rank and file, as always, have the basic Russian qualities of toughness and stubbornness. Their technical education has no doubt improved beyond recognition, but there is no evidence that this has remotely matched that of their Western counterparts. The Russian soldier's mental processes are slow on the battlefield and initiative is not his strong point. If he is left leaderless or without orders he will do very little. For these reasons it appears that unit for unit, the West has a decided advantage in quality.

Any conjectures regarding possible future operations by the Red Army in Europe must be based upon the type of equipment and training currently in use and being practised.

It is fair to assume that in the event of an open conflict between NATO and Warsaw Pact countries, the latter are planning upon

[Imperial War Museum

Fire and movement. A T34 "shoots in" its attendant infantry into a village

a strategic offensive to the West. Their armament is basically offensive, and is shown by the production of vast quantities of amphibious tanks and APCs, to be used, presumably, in breaching the successive river lines upon which NATO defensives could be based.

[Imperial War Museum

A reconnaissance on foot by vehicle commanders from a troop of BT7s

As so much of their training takes place at night (one estimate puts it at two-thirds), it is obviously their intention to fight what is called the continuous 24-hour battle, in which units keep up an incessant round the clock pressure against the enemy until relieved or destroyed, the object being to wear down and demoralise the smaller NATO forces until they finally collapse. It is also expected that these tactics will be accompanied by massive infiltration, causing disruption and confusion in the NATO rear areas.

Of course, they have had ample opportunity to rehearse all this in detail over the last twenty years. As all vehicles are now fitted with radio, they have in theory, the flexibility to carry out their design. However, as any suitable concentration of vehicles will inevitably receive delivery of a NATO tactical nuclear missile, the execution of this design may prove impossible, as to fight efficiently armour must fight together and in quantity. It is also anticipated that the NATO armour, basically better in quality though fewer in numbers, is capable of giving its Communist counterpart a very bloody nose indeed.

Moreover, the logistic problems of such a massive undertaking are enormous, and one wonders whether, if one were a Russian, one would be happy about supply lines being secure whilst crossing such countries as Hungary and Czechoslovakia.

I feel that whilst the overall picture remains grey, it is by no means black, although continuing reduction in our armed forces may make it so if we continue to pander to the peculiar doctrinal fantasies of the Left.

Conclusion

The Soviet Armoured Corps has been fortunate in that, at its birth, it was unfettered by the traditions of another age and was therefore able to develop its theories in relative isolation, whilst absorbing the best of foreign technology.

Russian design philosophy has always shown clarity of purpose, and has taken full advantage of the massive productive capacity of the country in producing vehicles designed for different functions which can utilise the same basic components, thus enabling long, and therefore inexpensive, production runs. Designs have always proved to be robust and simple, vehicle crews therefore requiring the minimum of training. The Russian best is what is good enough for the job, and anything else is considered to be wasted effort.

The Red Army's appreciation of the potential of armour was evident early, and experience gained in the development of amphibious and air-portable vehicles in the 1930s has led to the production of the vast fleet of vehicles in those classes possessed by the Soviet Union today.

Russian designers have, until recently, been able to boast that, vehicle for vehicle, their tanks have had the advantage of a superior gun, but for the present, their lead in this field seems to have been lost to Britain.

On the debit side, Russian AFVs suffer from a number of elementary faults which can have a profound effect upon a vehicle's performance in battle, and in general it is fair to say that these have long since been eliminated in Western designs. Tactics still appear to rely on rehearsals and brute force, and the command philosophy does little to encourage the initiative so essential in a mobile battle.

Whilst the British and German claim to have fought the first tank-against-tank duel at Villers-Bretotneux in 1918 is not in dispute, the first full scale tank battle belongs to the Red Army and to the Italians, when 70 Russian tanks were opposed by two Italian motorised divisions at Guadalajara in 1937, during the Spanish Civil War.

To the Russians also falls the distinction of having won the greatest tank battle in history. This was fought at Kursk, following the Stalingrad operations, and ended in the utter defeat of the last great Panzer offensive mounted on the Eastern Front.

Armoured troops hold an honoured place in Russian military society. Every September great celebrations take place on Soviet Tankman's Day. Last year many Soviet Tankmen celebrated the occasion in Prague.